The Unlimited Sky Among Clouds
by Alexander Kishinevsky

Order this book online at www.trafford.com
or email orders@trafford.com

Most Trafford titles are also available at major online book retailers.

Printed in the United States of America.

ISBN: 978-1-4669-7731-0 (sc)
        978-1-4669-7730-3 (e)
Library of Congress Control Number: 2013901383

Trafford rev. 02/18/2013

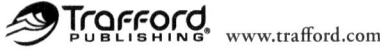 www.trafford.com

North America & international
toll-free: 1 888 232 4444 (USA & Canada)
phone: 250 383 6864 ♦ fax: 812 355 4082

Dedicated to my family and friends

Photos by Alexander Kishinevsky

Sky Base Universe

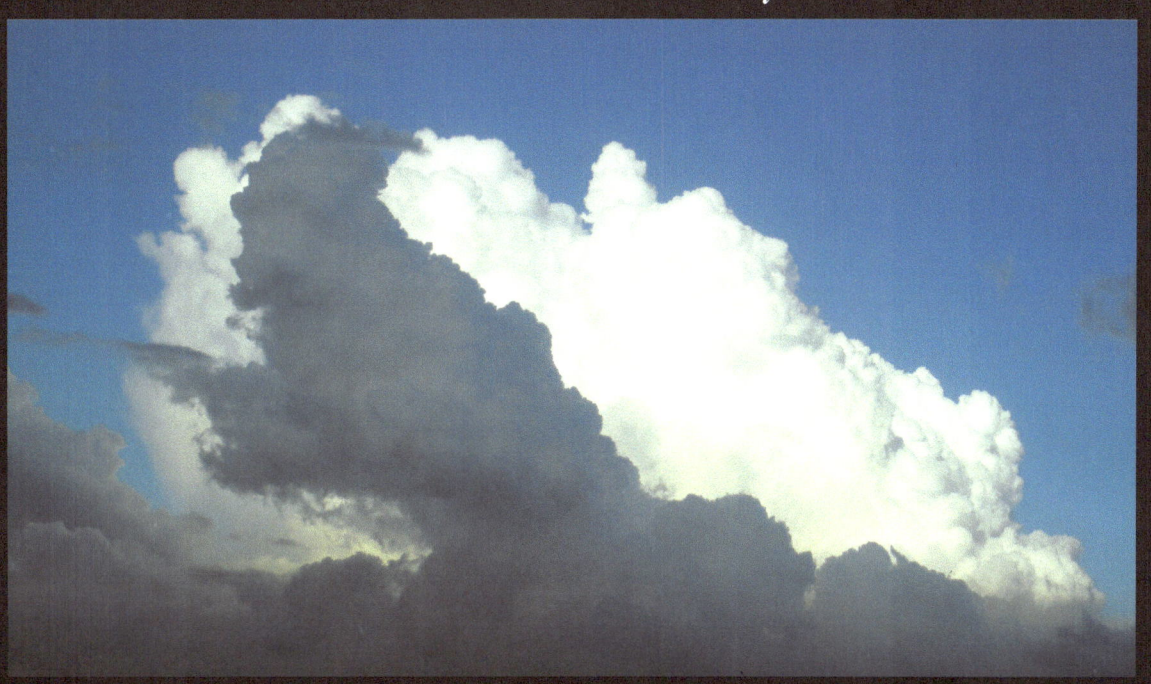

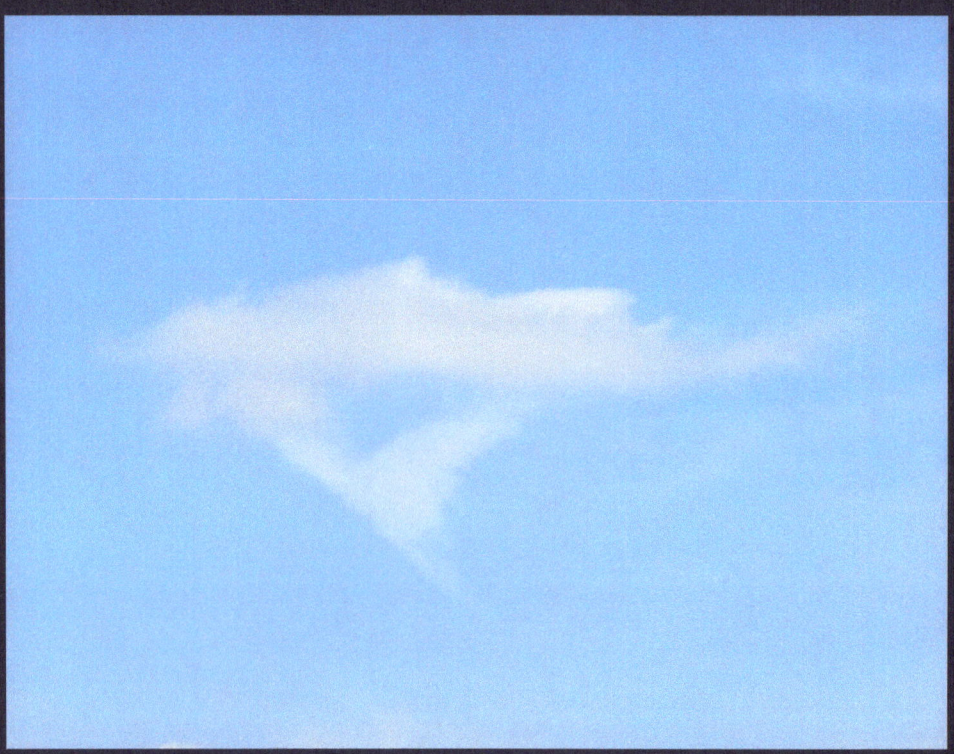

Sky Trek Enterprise 2014

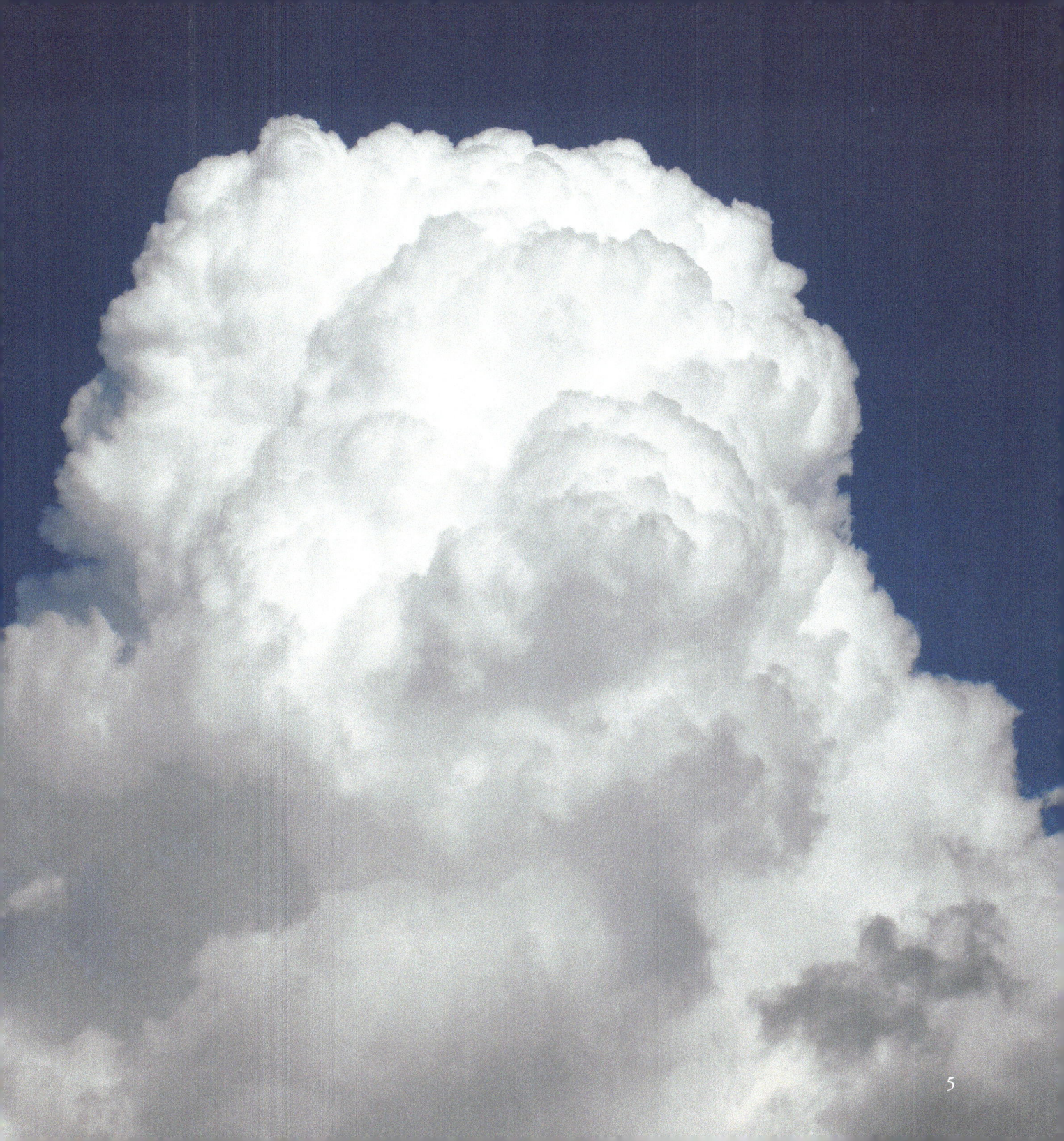

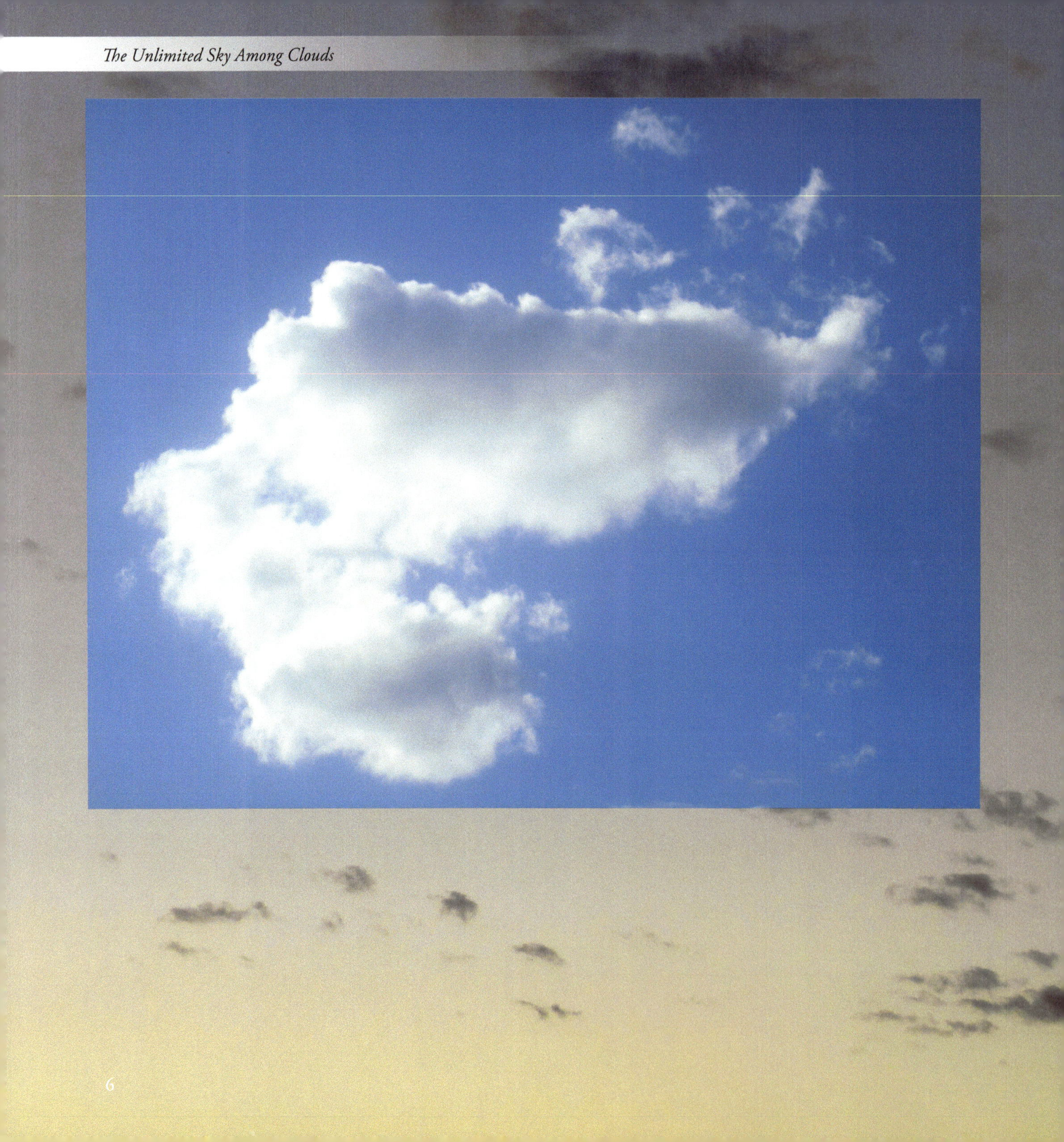

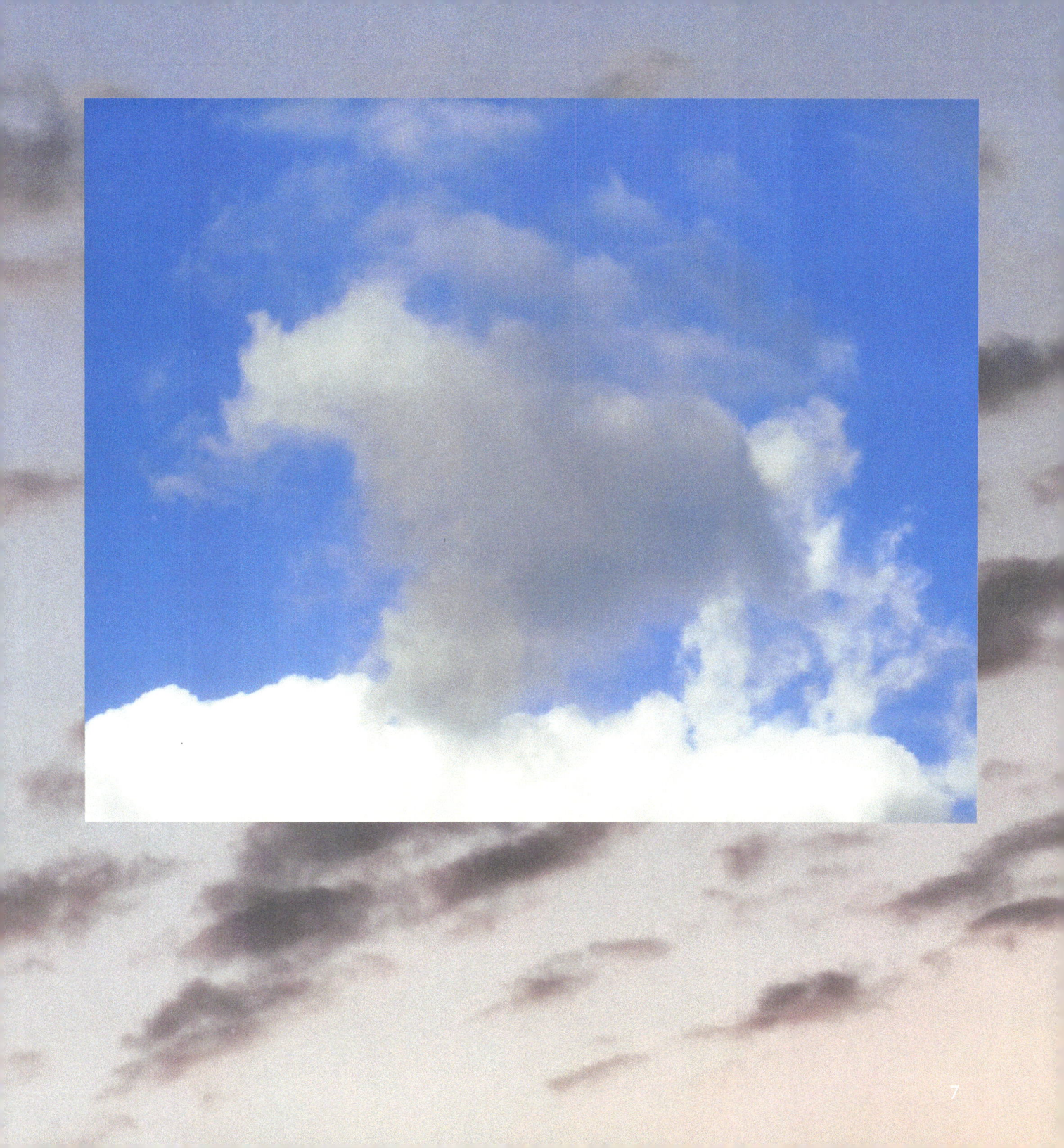

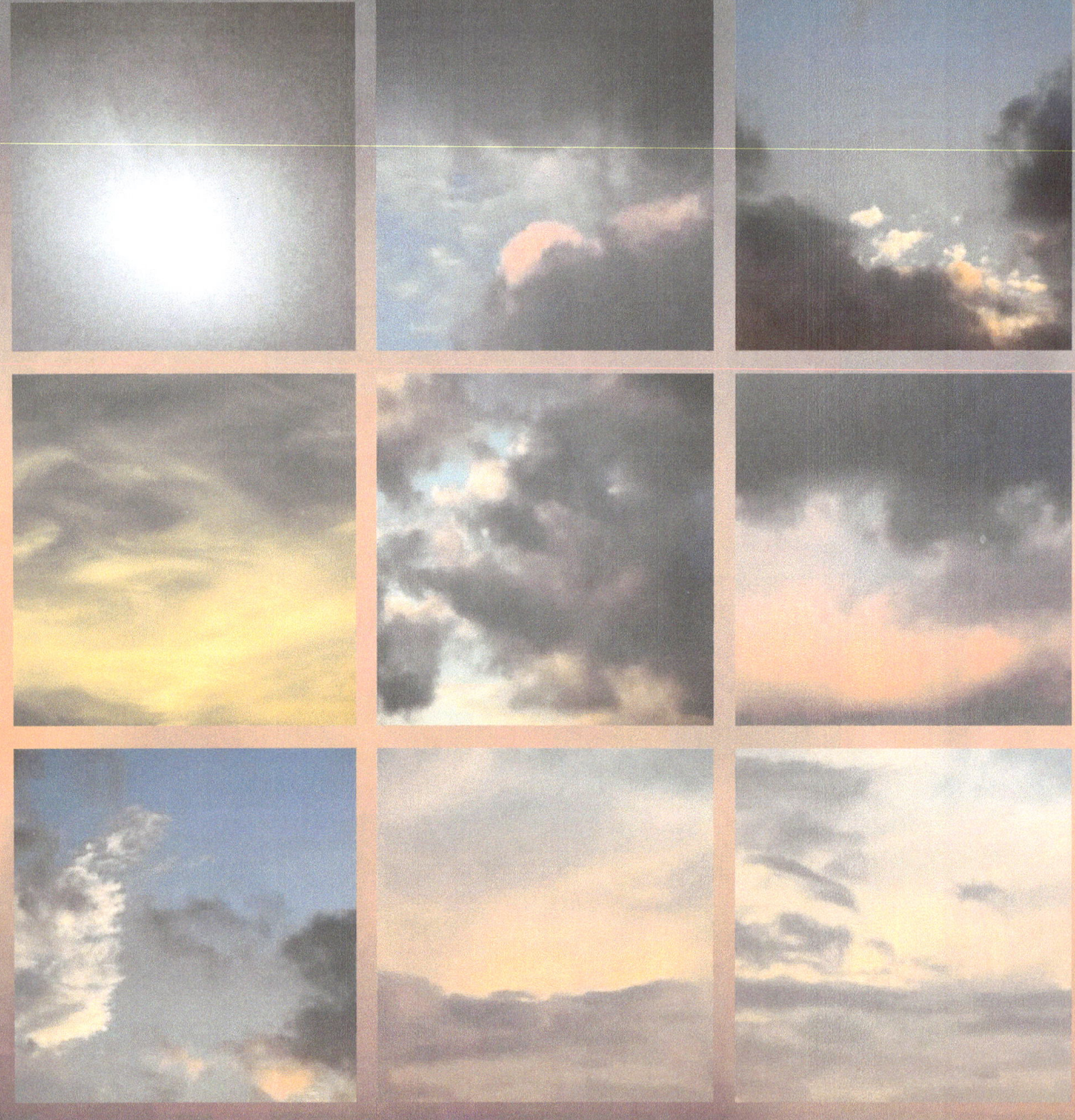

Sunrise or Sunset

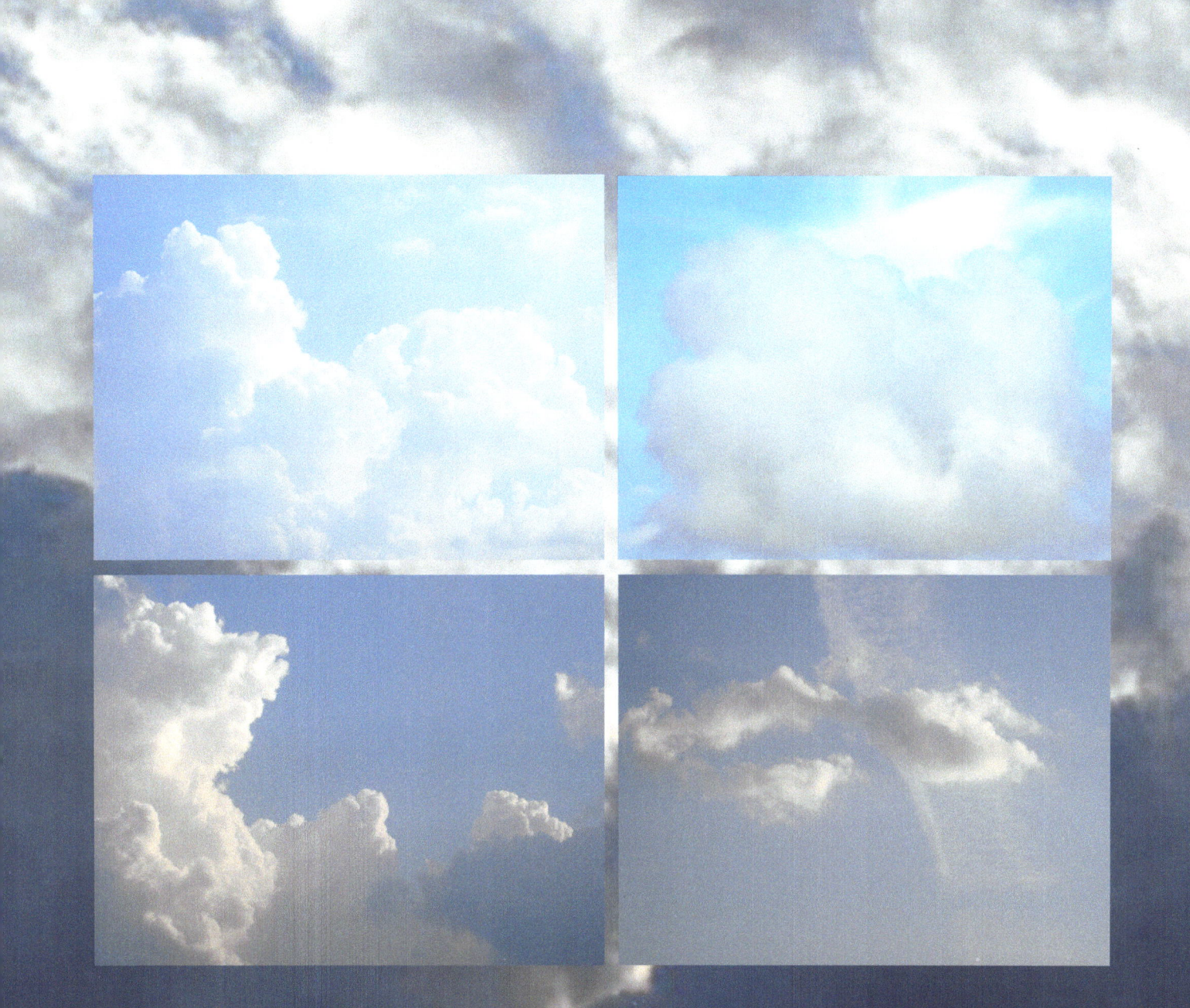

Cumulus Clouds

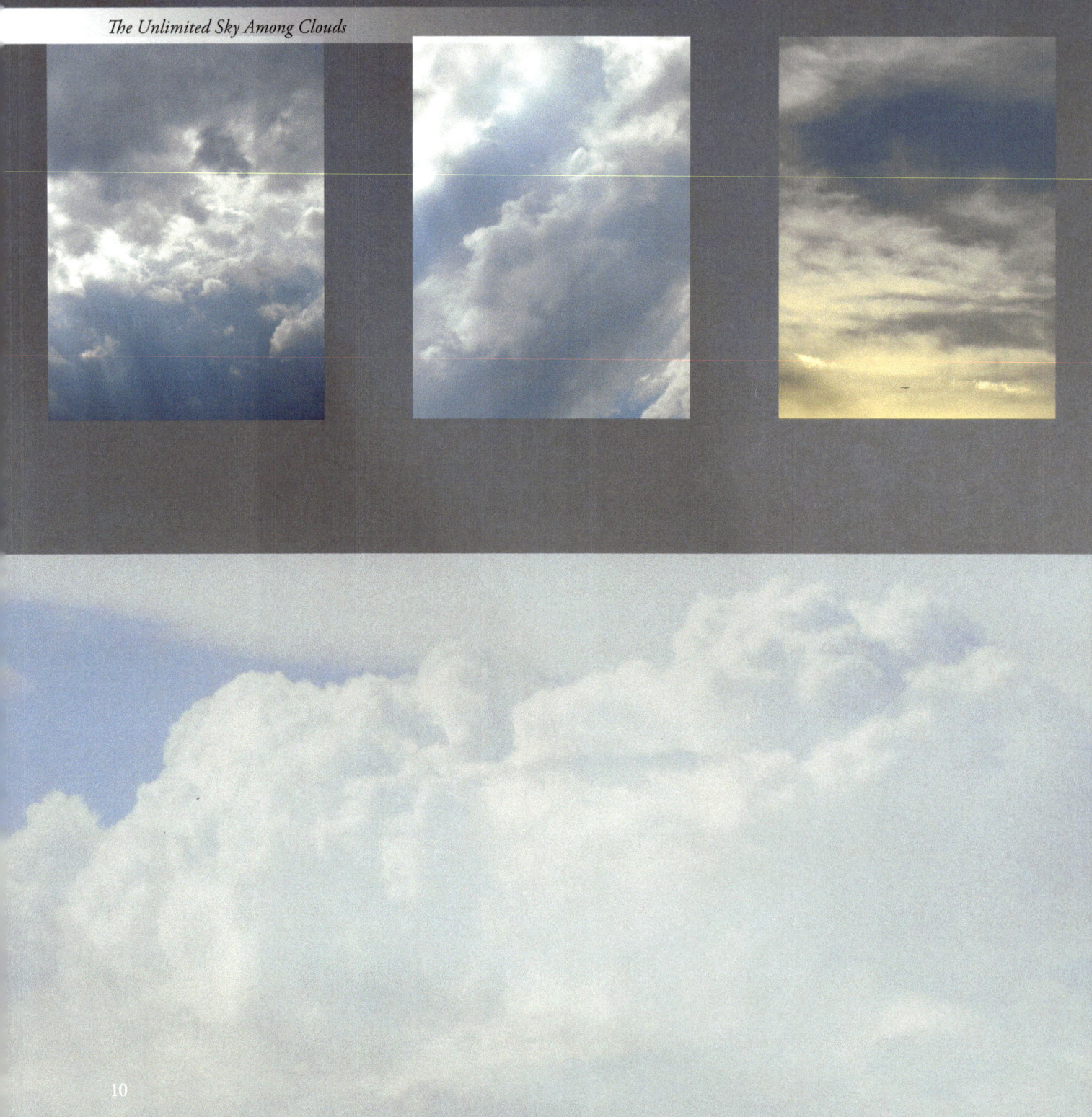

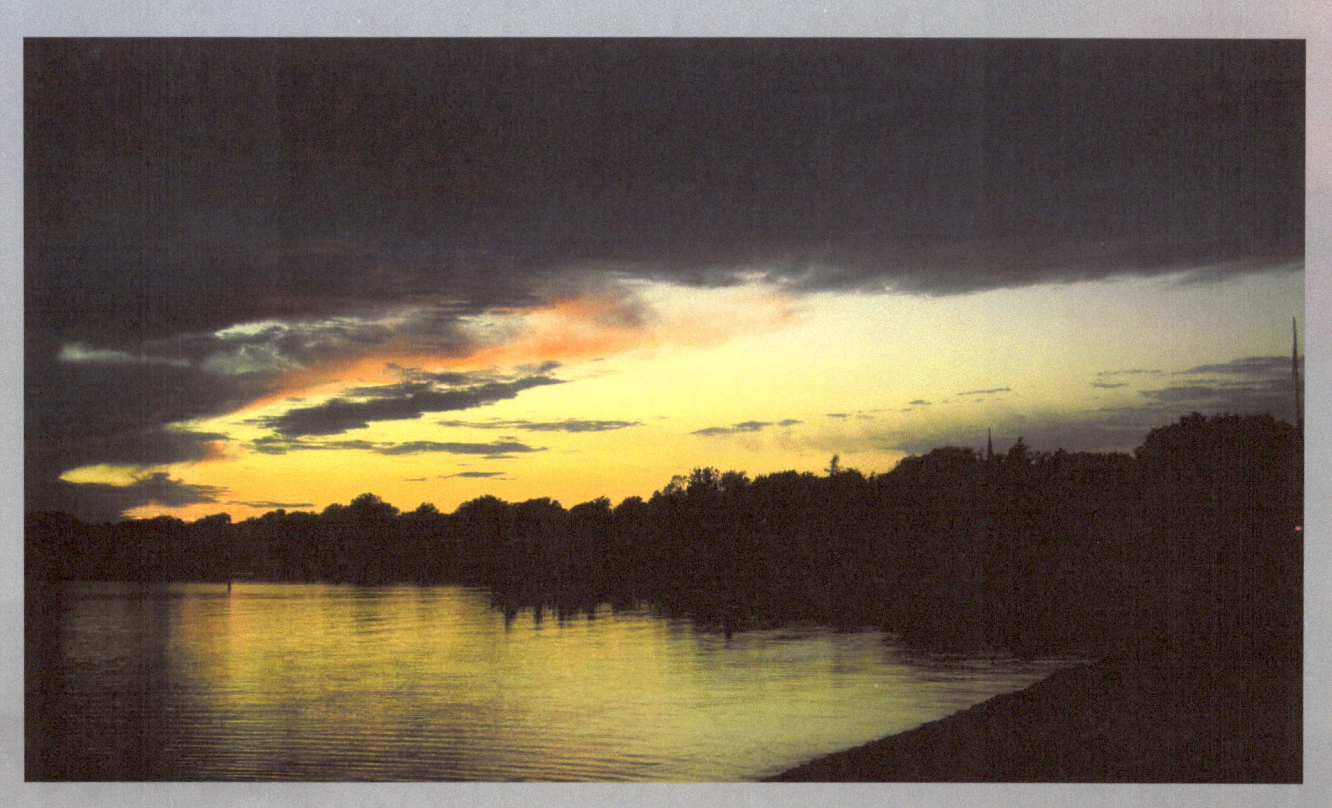

Lake in Wisconsin, USA

WILLIAMSBURG, VA, USA

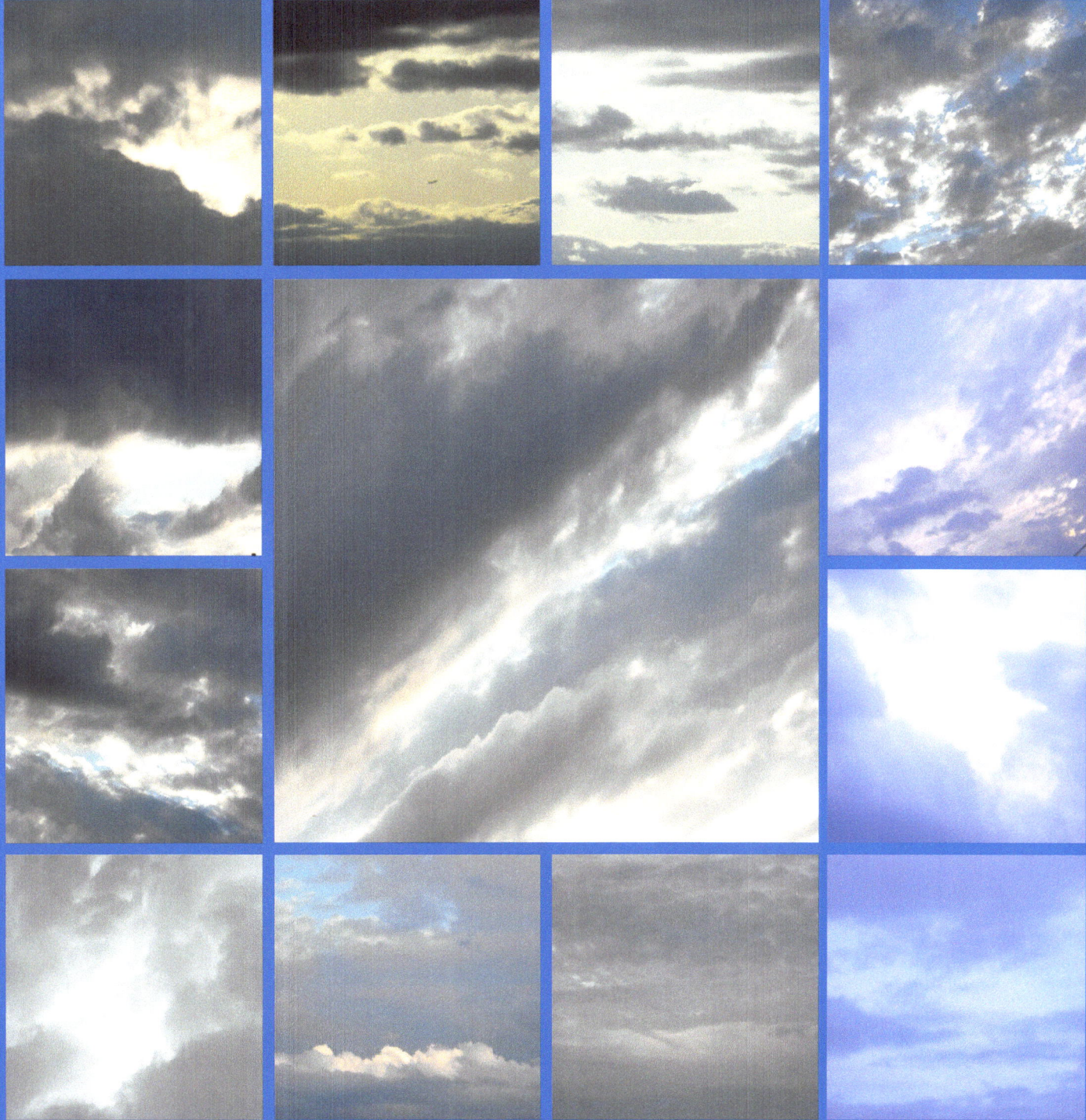

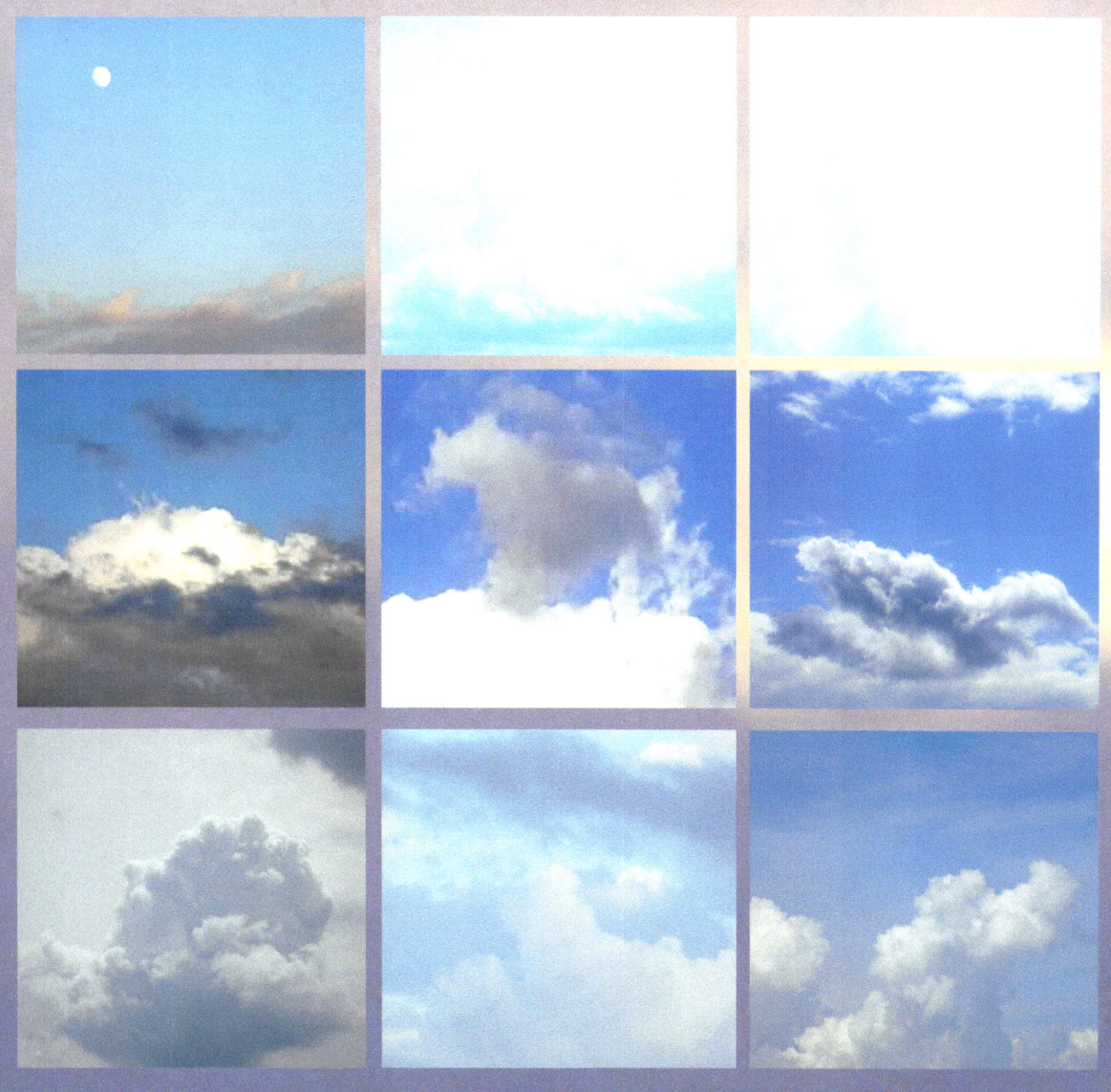

Photos by Alexander Kishinevsky

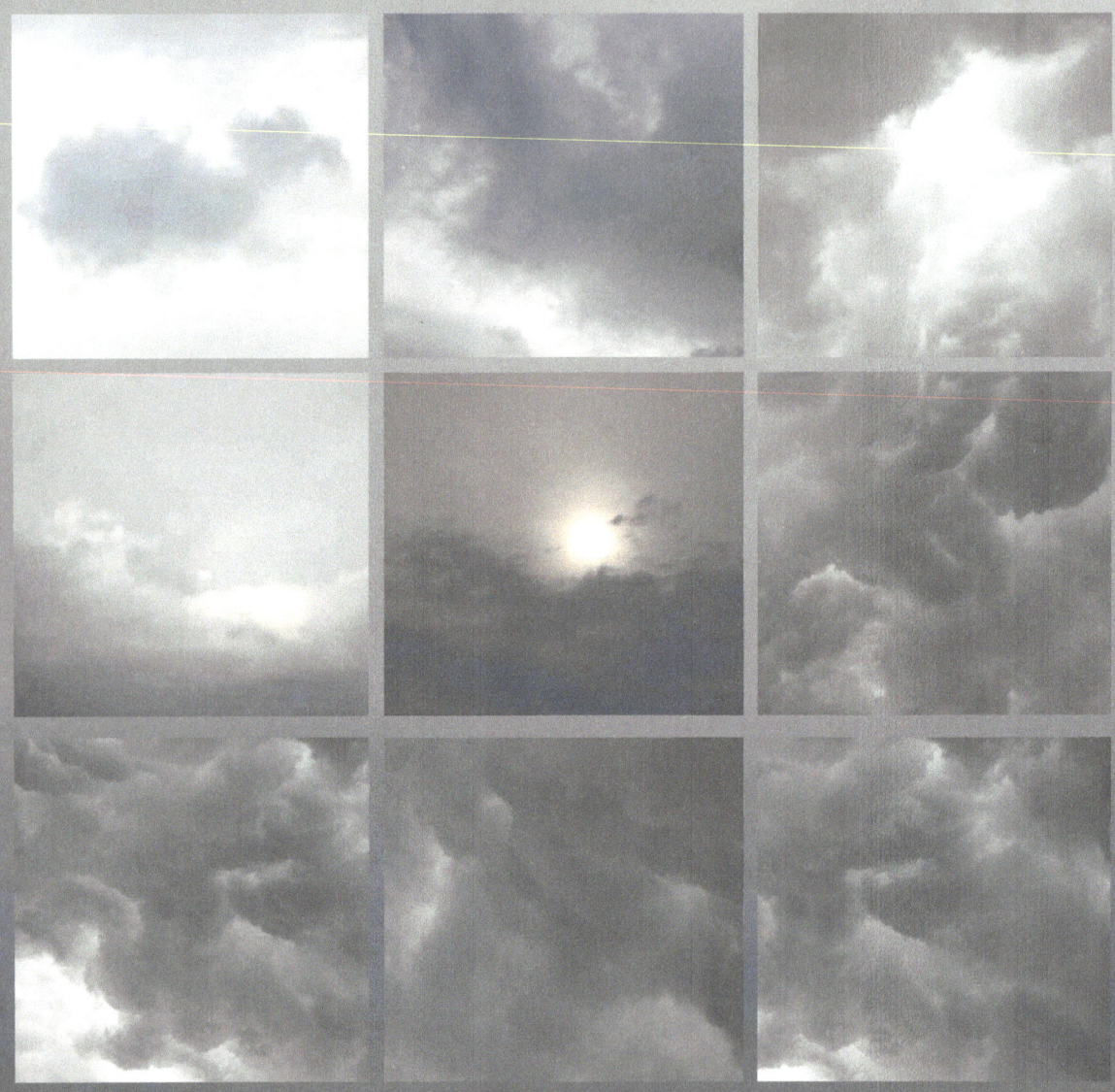

Ash Clouds

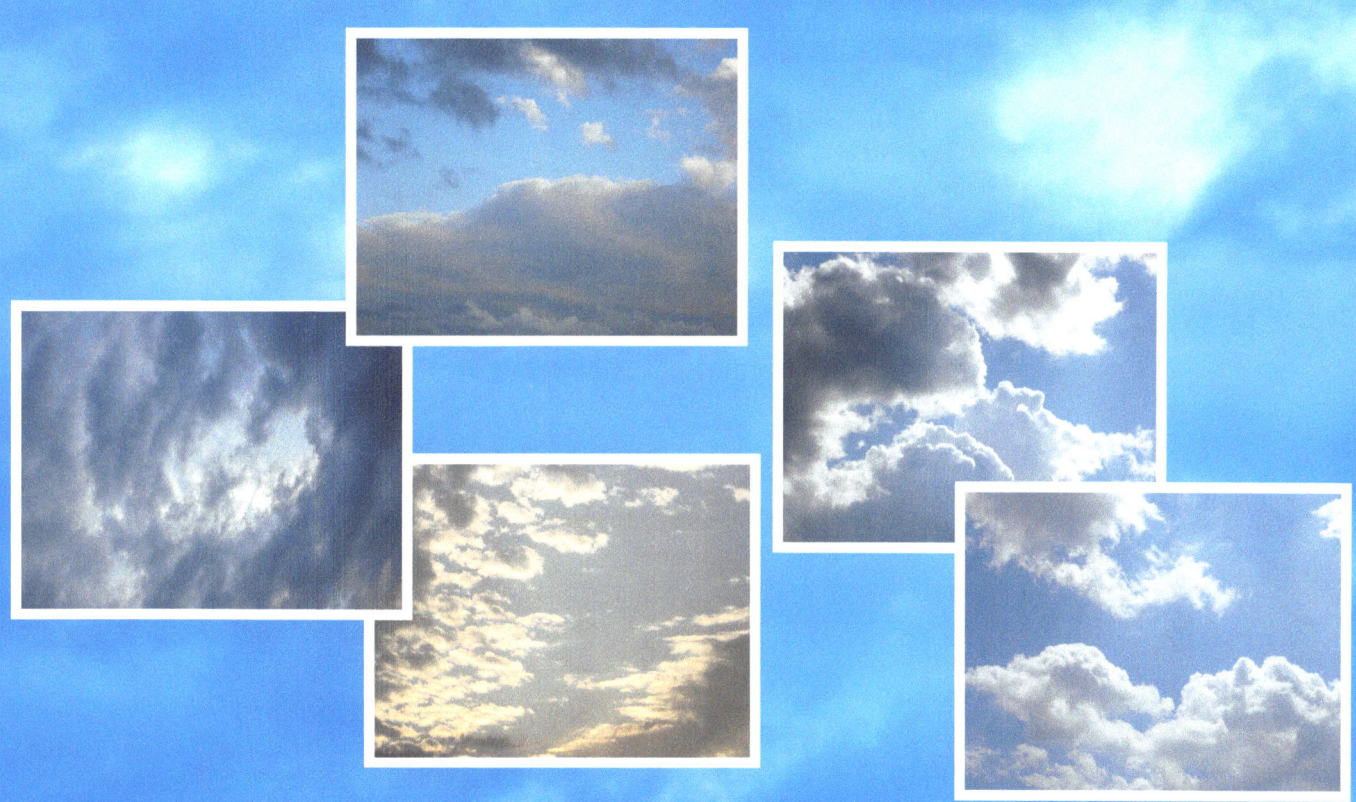

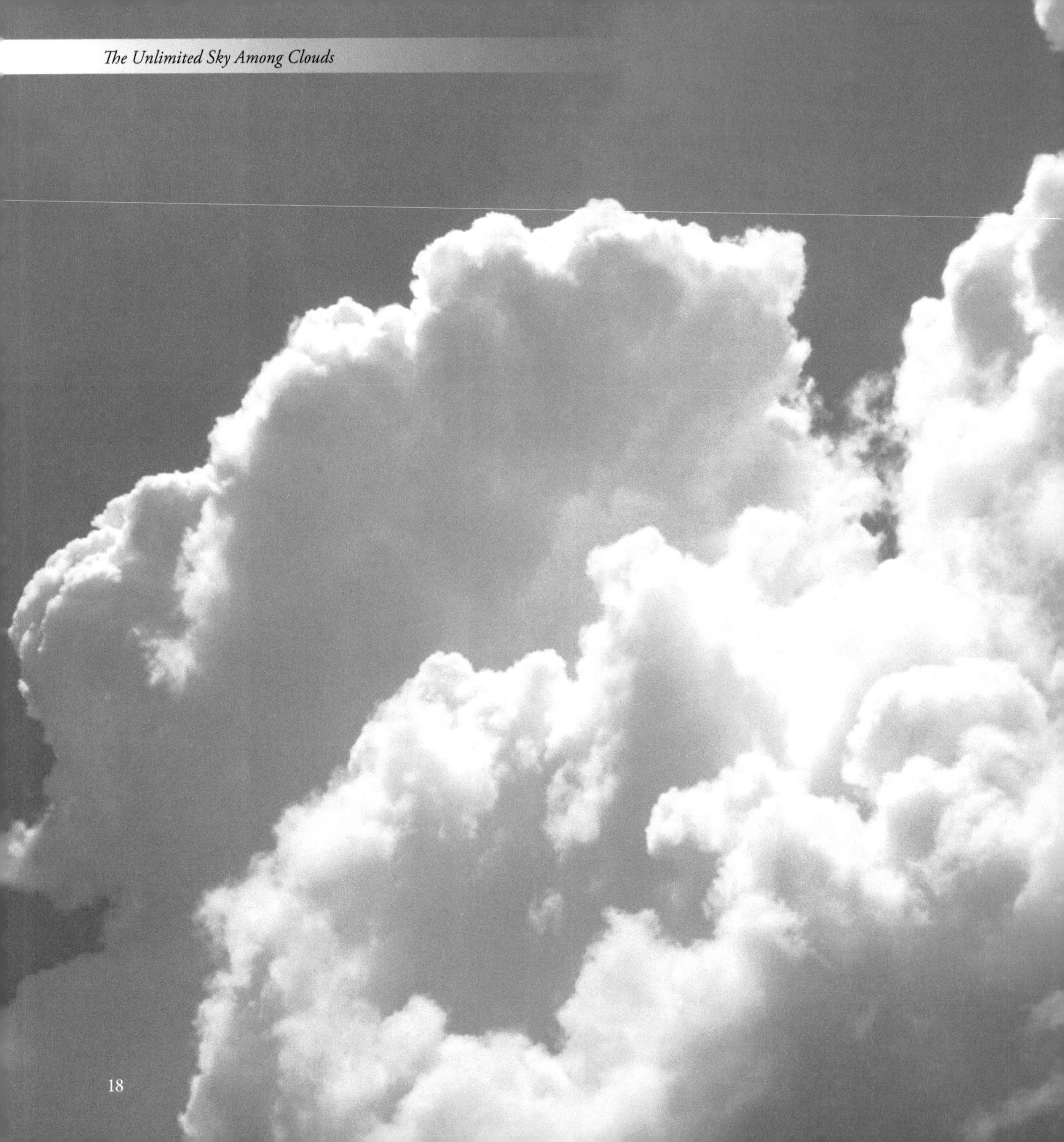

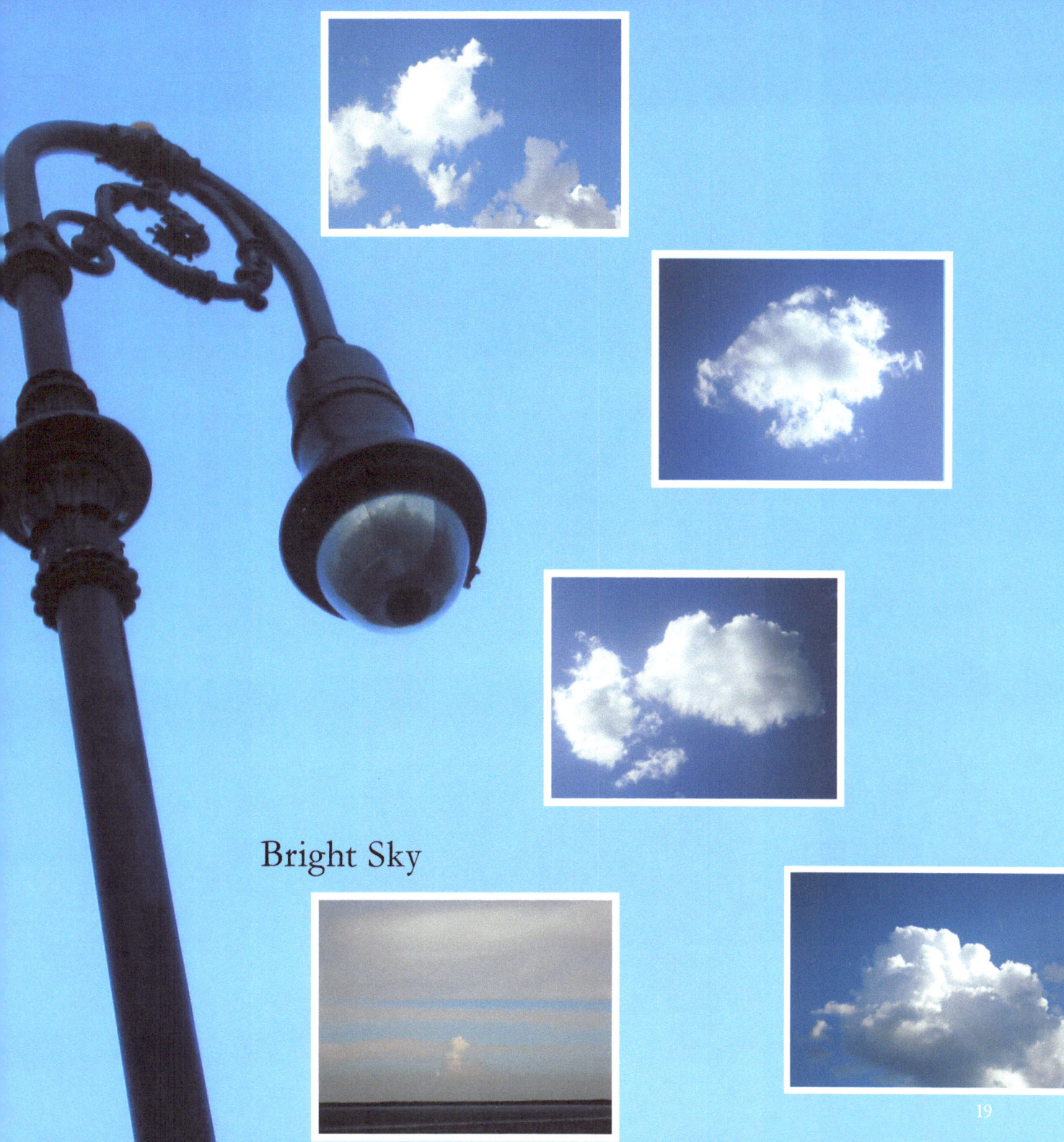

Bright Sky

19

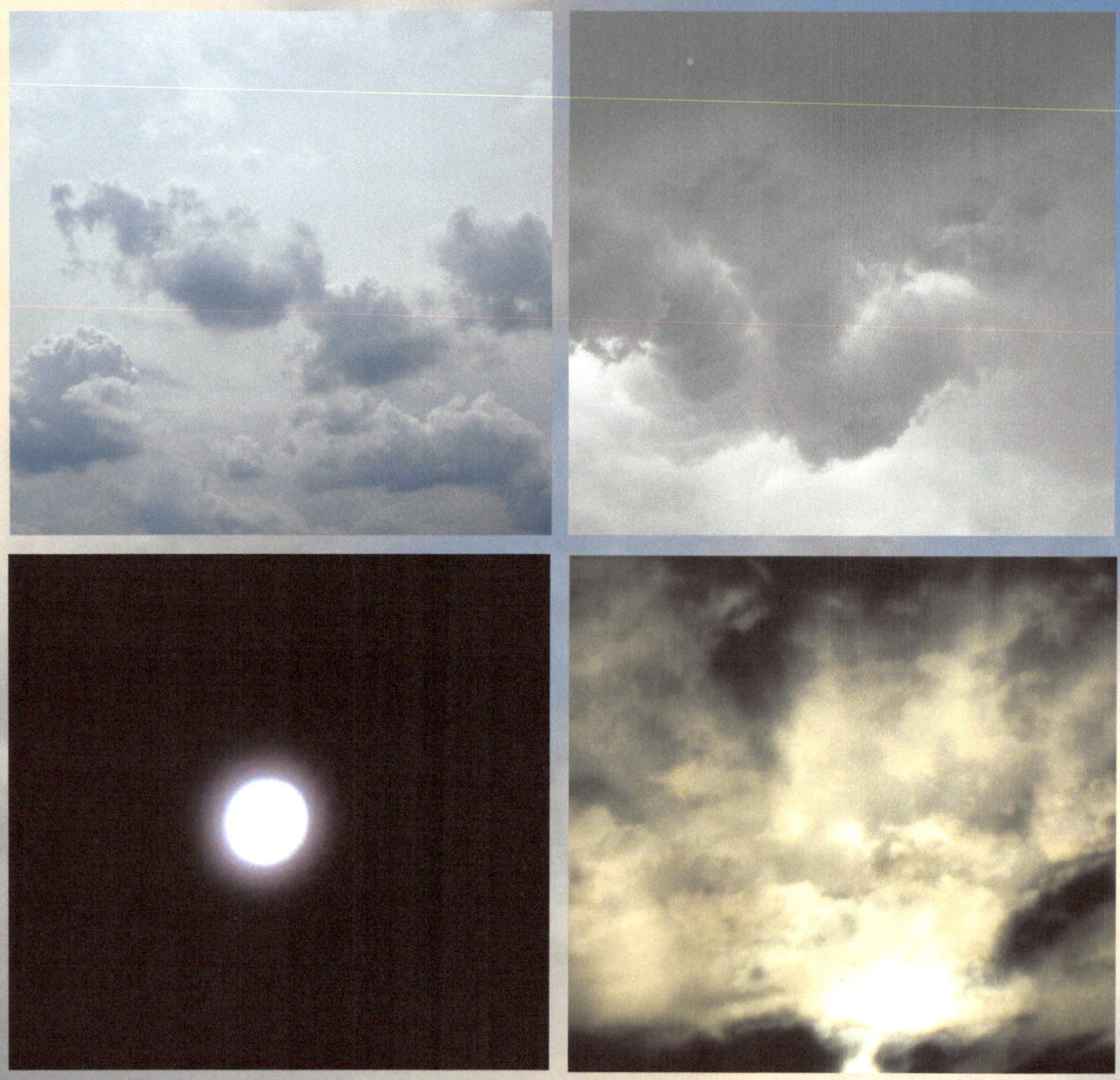

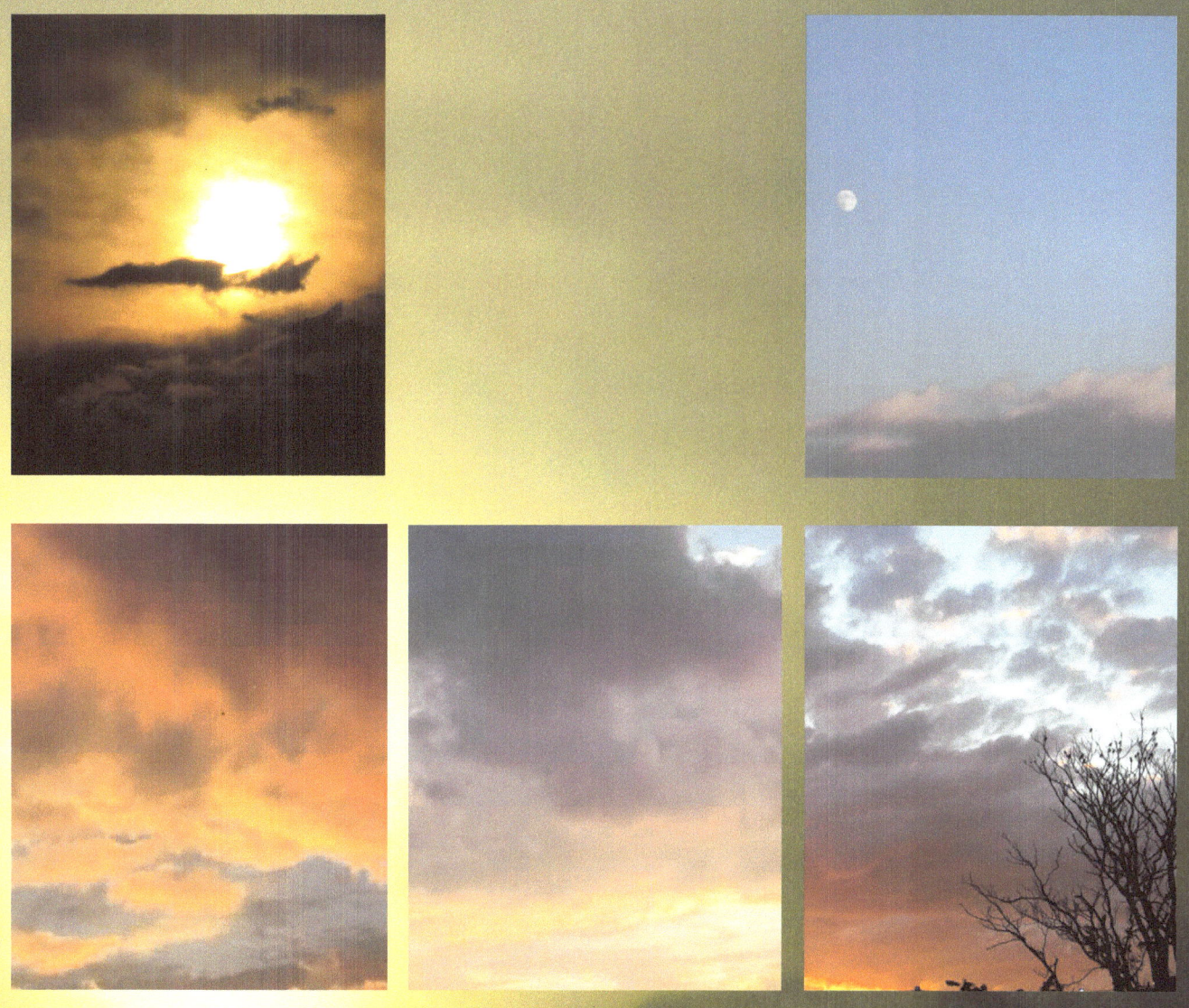

Gone with the Wind

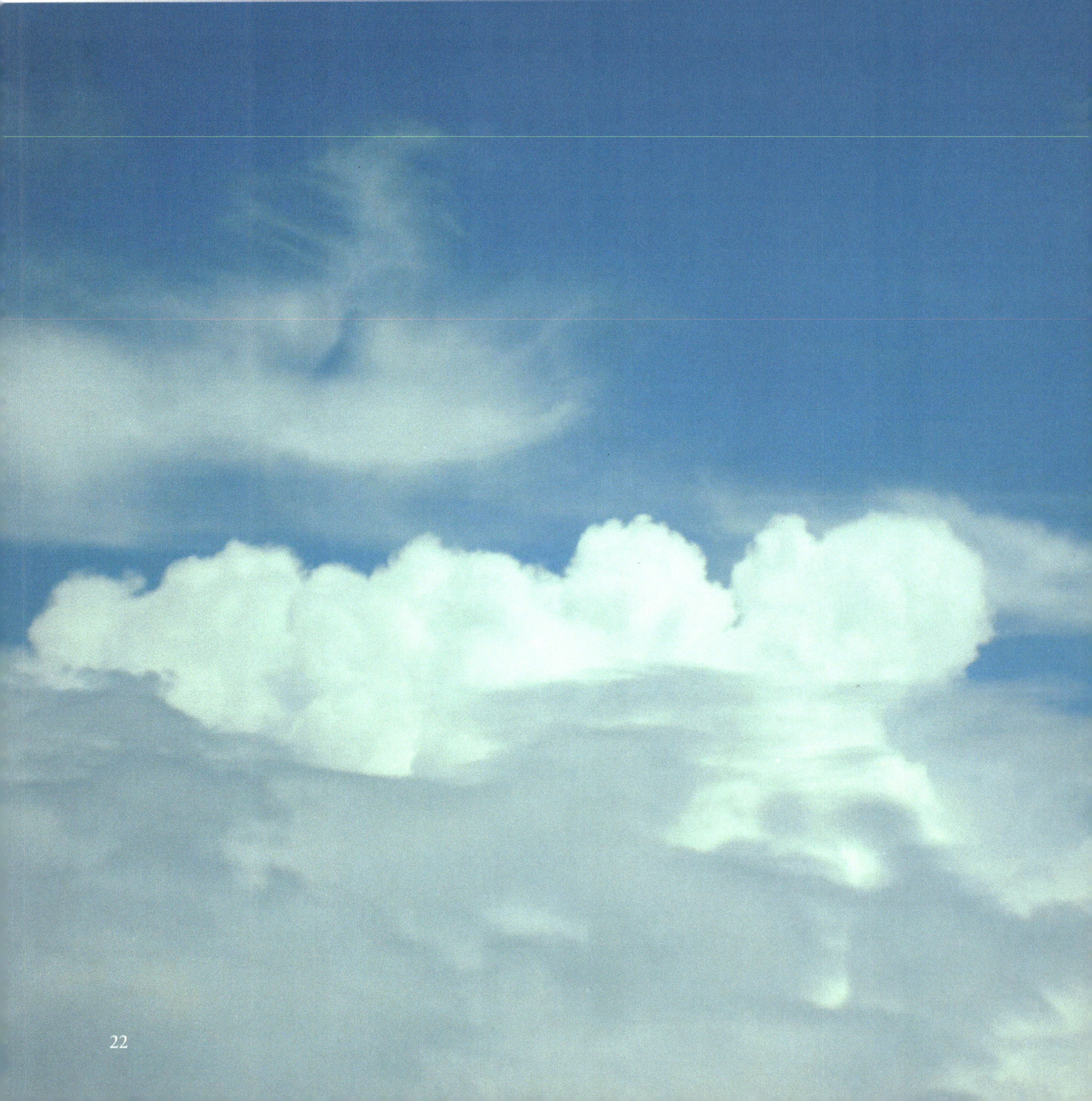

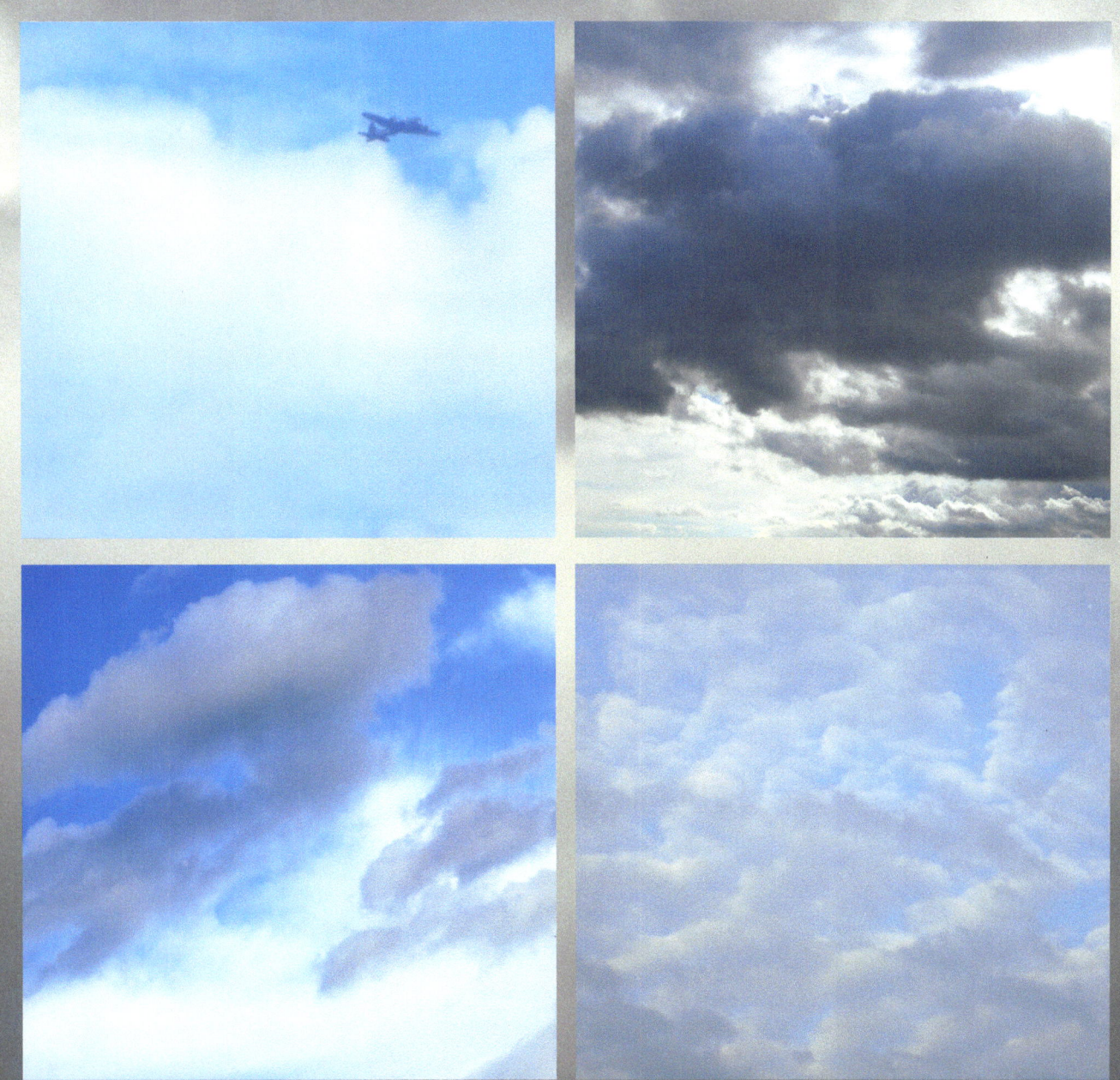

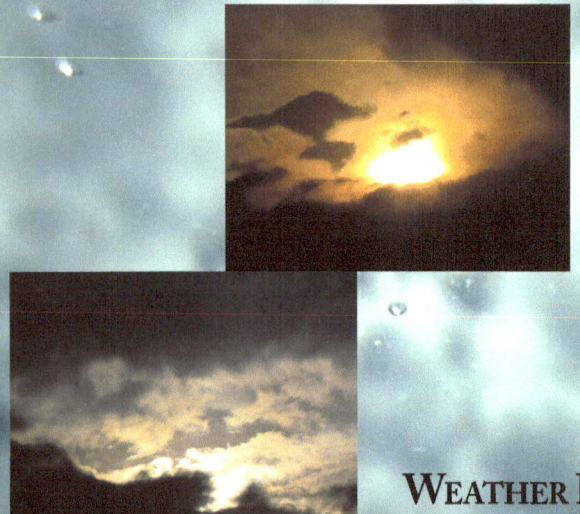

WEATHER FROM THE WINDOW

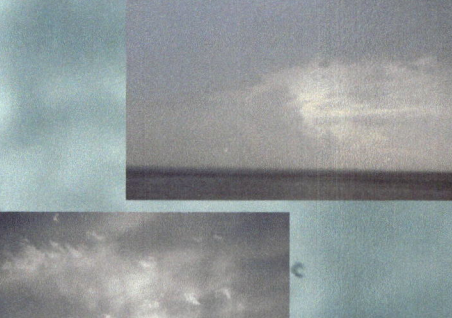

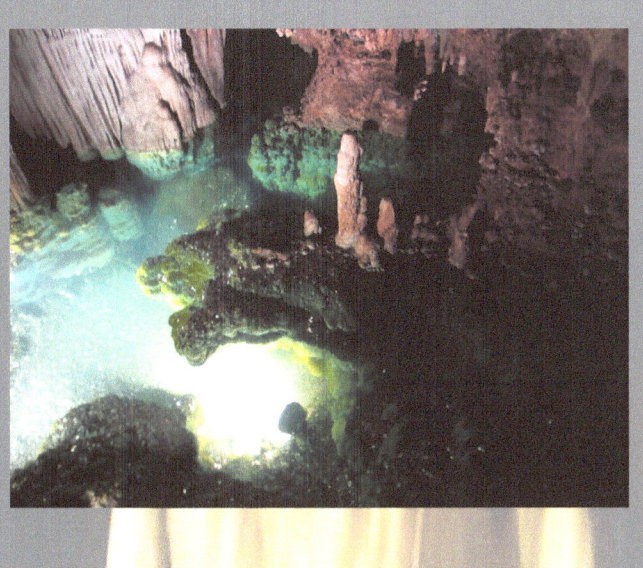

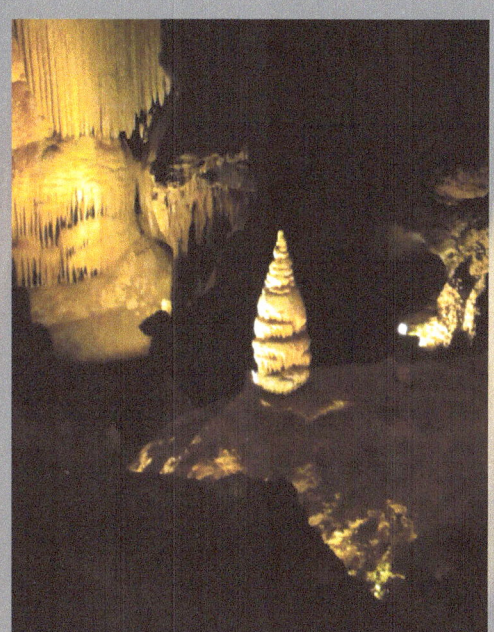

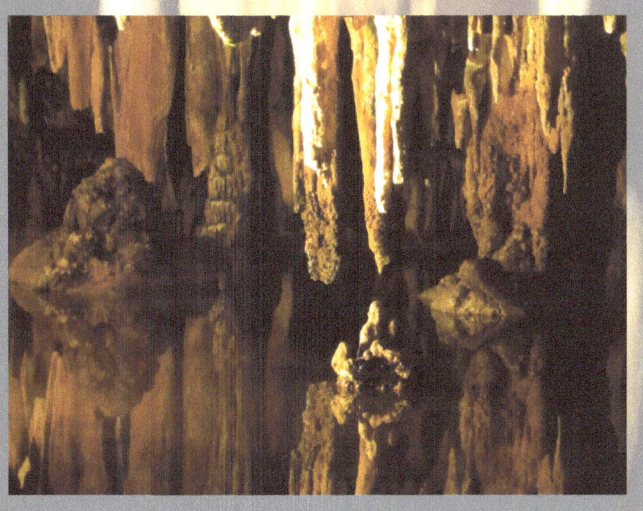

Beauty under Mountains

www.ingramcontent.com/pod-product-compliance
Lightning Source LLC
Chambersburg PA
CBHW050427180526

45159CB00005B/2447